DISCOVERING
ENERGY

Button BOOKS

EDUARD ALTARRIBA

JOHANNES HIRN & VERONICA SANZ

Contents

The universe is filled with billions of galaxies, which are each made up of billions of stars. Inside stars, very tiny particles bump into each other and release an incredibly powerful source of energy, which is how things move and change. This energy then escapes in the form of light and other particles that travel through space.

One of these stars, our Sun, is the source of all energy for life on Earth, despite being millions of miles away from us. This energy makes plants grow, and these plants then feed animals. The Sun's energy is also locked within petroleum, coal, and natural gas, and humans have found clever ways to release this energy.

Thanks to science, sunlight can also be harnessed to produce electricity. The Sun's heat also causes winds, which we can use to produce electricity too. In this book, you will learn about the many exciting ways that energy affects our lives.

The Sun's energy

The energy from the Sun is necessary for all living beings on Earth to exist. Energy from the Sun travels 93 million miles across space and gives us our natural heat and light. When the heat from the Sun gets to Earth, gases in our air trap that heat, acting like a greenhouse. These are known as **greenhouse gases** and **carbon dioxide** (CO_2) is one of the main greenhouse gases.

Plants

Most plants use sunlight, water, and CO_2 gas from the air to grow. This is called PHOTOSYNTHESIS. The trees and other plants use sunlight to make sugar and other materials to help them grow.

Animals

All animals eat plants or other animals. Animals use the energy stored in plants to help them grow and move. This energy is stored in the animal until needed or, if it is eaten by another animal, it is stored in that animal. The chemical reactions involved in digestion and **BREATHING** release some of the CO_2 from the plants back into the air.

Fire

More than one million years ago early humans started using fire to warm themselves, cook, and keep dangerous animals away. BURNING plants in the form of wood or charcoal releases their CO_2 back into the atmosphere, in much the same way that breathing does.

5

Muscular energy

The muscles in our bodies help us to move. They do this by pulling and contracting, or shortening. We call this **tension**. When this tension is released, the muscle returns to its resting length and the bone it is attached to moves. This muscular energy is how we move our legs, arms, and everything else to perform physical tasks.

Early humans built their shelters using **MUSCLE MOVEMENTS**. Modern humans do the same, but they can now use machines to do tasks quicker.

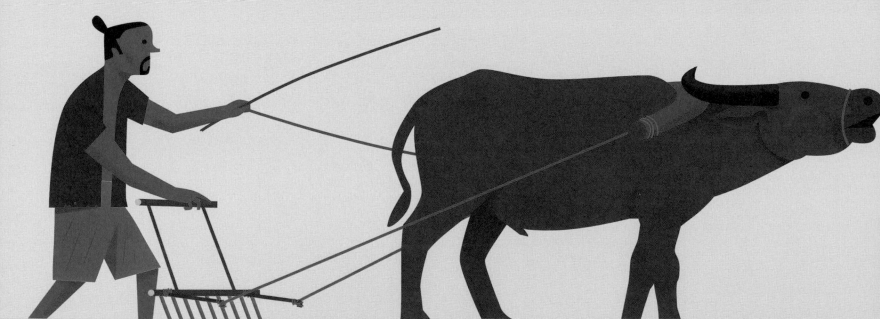

Humans figured out they could make **ANIMALS** work for them. Horses could be ridden to get to places faster than any human could run. Oxen could pull heavy plows that a person could not move. These animals are bigger than people, so their muscles are larger, and they can store more energy than us.

What is energy?

ARISTOTLE

Scientists say **WORK** is done when a force applied to an object makes that object move. When you apply a force, by kicking a ball, for instance, you move the ball. People who sit in meetings using big words aren't doing actual "work," but they still call it that.

People have always known that things move, but for a long time, no one knew how or why. Aristotle, the clever ancient Greek, realized that sometimes nothing is happening, but it might. This is called **POTENTIAL**. So a ball that is not moving has the potential to roll down a hill. Aristotle gave the name **ENERGY** to this **CAPACITY TO PRODUCE WORK**.

Potential and kinetic energy

Aristotle also spotted that the bent bow of an archer holds potential. When the archer releases the pulled string, the **POTENTIAL ENERGY** propels the arrow forward at a mighty speed (if the archer is any good). This released energy is now called **KINETIC ENERGY**.

The potential energy is held in the bow, as long as it is kept bent. It can be released at any time by letting go of the string. Then the energy of the bow is transmitted to the arrow, and the bow has done its work.

Centuries of sailing

As far as we know, the first sails were used about 5,500 years ago on the River Nile. Egyptian sailors wanting to power their boats would move their sails so that as much of the sail as possible faced the wind. The wind pushing into the sail created higher pressure on that side. The sail, and therefore the whole boat, then moved from the high-pressure area to the lower-pressure area.

Harnessing the wind

From Egyptian boats using a simple square sail to huge merchant ships made of steel with up to five masts, sailors have been harnessing the wind to move their ships across the surface of seas, rivers, and oceans to explore, trade, fight, and have fun.

Long ago, sailors prayed to gods asking for wind to help move their boats. We now know that wind is caused by the Sun's heat setting air in motion.

WINDS CHANGE SPEED, STRENGTH, AND DIRECTION, SO SAILORS HAVE ALWAYS NEEDED TO KEEP TRACK OF THEM.

N
NW   NE
W   E
SW   SE
S

USING THE
wind

Millstones are heavy stones that are used to grind wheat into flour. Rather than tire themselves or their animals moving the stones, people realized they could use the wind's power, thanks to a clever machine called the windmill.

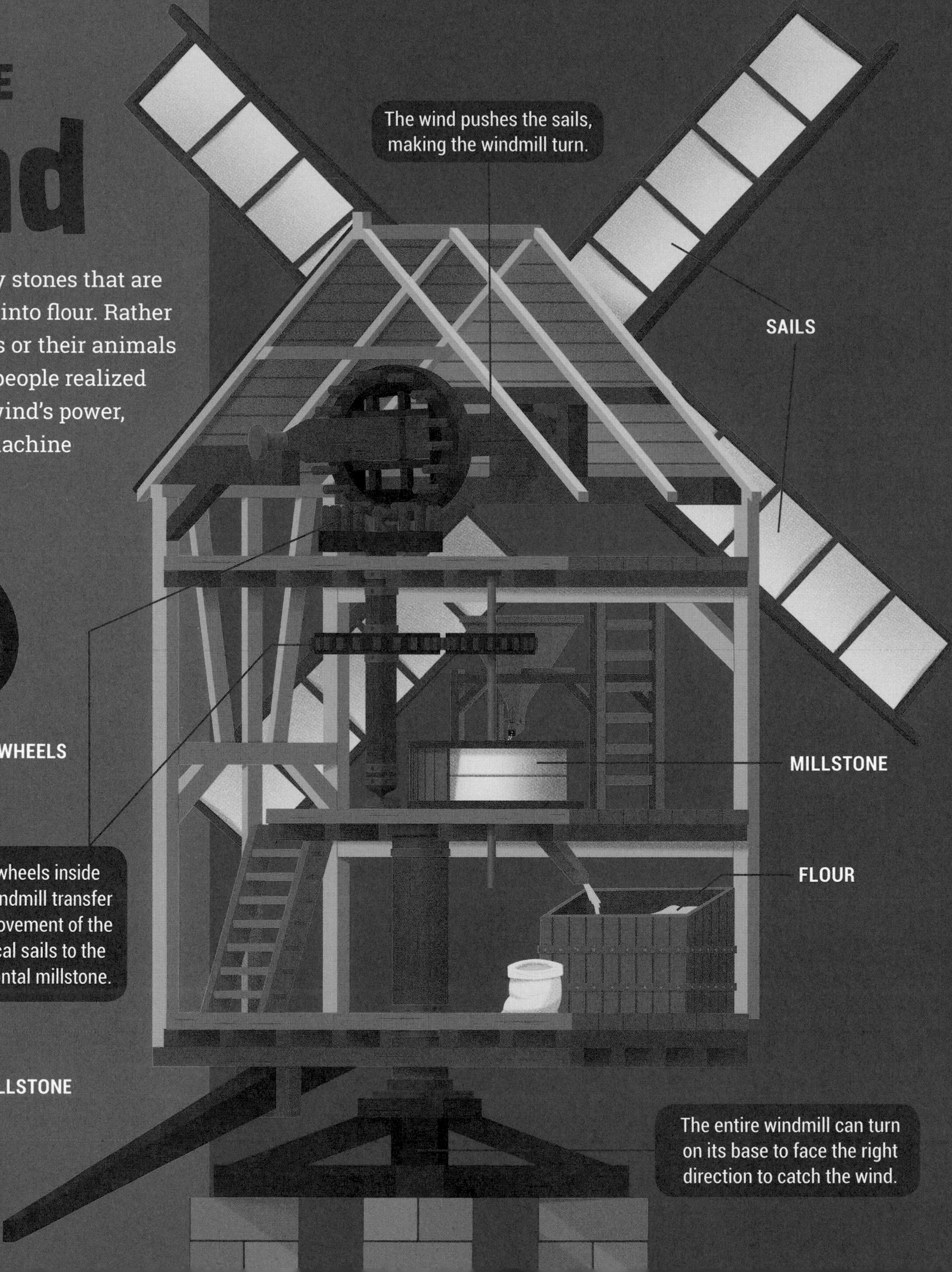

The wind pushes the sails, making the windmill turn.

SAILS

COGWHEELS

Cogwheels inside the windmill transfer the movement of the vertical sails to the horizontal millstone.

MILLSTONE

FLOUR

MILLSTONE

The entire windmill can turn on its base to face the right direction to catch the wind.

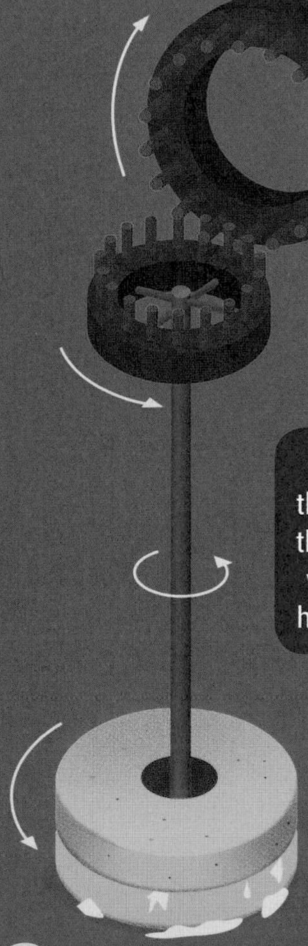

ATMOSPHERE

IS THERE WIND ON THE MOON?

Although we may think of air as empty space, it actually contains GASES such as nitrogen, oxygen, and water vapor. There is air in the atmosphere around Earth, but there is no atmosphere around the Moon. This means that there is nothing to blow around and cause wind.

When the Apollo mission astronauts planted a flag on the Moon's surface, they added a rod along the top edge to hold the flag out, otherwise it would have drooped downward. Without any wind to move it, the flag didn't flutter.

Water power

Dams are giant walls put across rivers to stop them flowing. The lake that builds up behind a dam then has **potential energy**. When the dam is open, water flows downward under the pull of Earth's **gravity**. Gravity is the force pulling everything down toward the ground. Just like animals and dropped ice cream, water is pulled down by gravity too. As the water flows, it gets faster and can push objects by **transferring energy** to them.

A watermill can transform water's flow into a CIRCULAR motion, which can then be used in machines similar to the windmill. Thanks to watermills, we can harness the energy in the flow of rivers and streams.

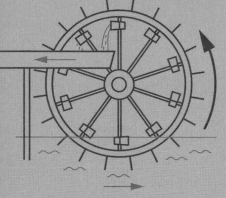

USING RIVER FLOW
TO RAISE WATER

USING GRAVITY TO
POWER A WATER WHEEL

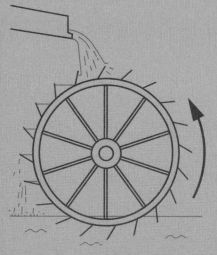

WATER WHEEL

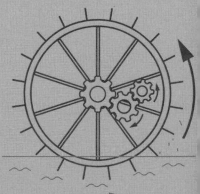

USING RIVER FLOW TO
POWER MACHINERY

USING RIVER FLOW
TO SPIN GEARS

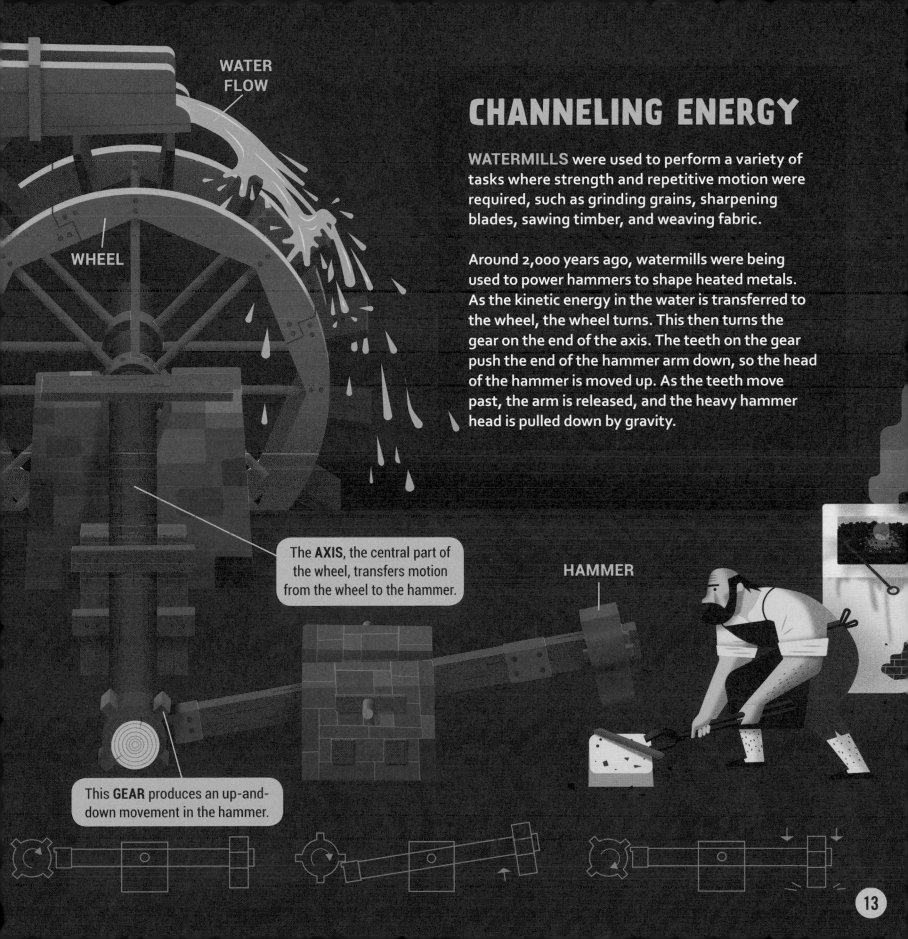

WATER FLOW

WHEEL

CHANNELING ENERGY

WATERMILLS were used to perform a variety of tasks where strength and repetitive motion were required, such as grinding grains, sharpening blades, sawing timber, and weaving fabric.

Around 2,000 years ago, watermills were being used to power hammers to shape heated metals. As the kinetic energy in the water is transferred to the wheel, the wheel turns. This then turns the gear on the end of the axis. The teeth on the gear push the end of the hammer arm down, so the head of the hammer is moved up. As the teeth move past, the arm is released, and the heavy hammer head is pulled down by gravity.

The **AXIS**, the central part of the wheel, transfers motion from the wheel to the hammer.

HAMMER

This **GEAR** produces an up-and-down movement in the hammer.

Math and mechanics

For a very long time, mathematics has been used in everyday life, for counting quantities of grain, oil, wine, and other valuable goods. It was also used to work out costs and payments. But people soon realized that the entire universe could be described through mathematics.

People have been studying the movements of stars and planets in the night sky for thousands of years. They spotted patterns and repetitions in these motions and started measuring the planets' positions with greater and greater accuracy. They then made models of the Solar System and astronomers tried to understand the patterns of the movements the planets were following.

Early scientists including GALILEO GALILEI and ISAAC NEWTON realized that the same laws of motion that ruled the planets would also affect objects on Earth. For instance, the force that causes apples to fall toward the ground on Earth is the same basic force that is responsible for the planets' motion around the Sun.

Science helped people understand how nature works. This knowledge meant engineers could invent many machines and devices that changed people's lives.

GALILEO

A PENDULUM is a weight that is hung up so that it can swing back and forth freely. Galileo used the regular motion of pendulums in his experiments to study timekeeping.

NEWTON

NEWTON came up with some basic laws of nature and expressed them in mathematical equations.

GALILEO also came up with ideas of ways to test what happens when things fall to Earth from a great height.

Clocks and robots

From the simple PENDULUM, complicated machines such as clocks and watches were created to measure time. Even ROBOTS that could perform mechanical tasks evolved from the pendulum.

These machines involved winding mechanisms to STORE energy, timers and buttons to RELEASE it, and gears to transmit MOTION to different parts.

Magic mechanism

The Turk was a device made around 1770 that appeared to play chess automatically and won many matches against the best players in Europe and America. Actually it was a trick, with a human chess master hiding inside, operating the mechanism. The use of gears to transmit motion made it look as if a life-sized model, dressed in traditional Turkish clothes, was moving the chess pieces.

Thermal energy

As the Sun comes up each morning, the environment warms up, and our bodies sense these changes in temperature. When we get too hot, we sweat to cool down. When the air is cold around us, our muscles shiver to warm us up. What we experience as heat and cold is just another form of energy, known as thermal energy.

WORKING IN A FORGE

A blacksmith uses coal to heat metals until they become soft enough to shape. Coal was originally plants from millions of years ago that stored energy from the Sun. Burning it releases this energy. The intense heat is then transferred to the metal, allowing the blacksmith to shape it into tools and machinery.

BELLOWS move air into the fire. The oxygen in the air helps things burn.

WHAT HAPPENS WHEN SOMETHING IS HEATED UP?

Everything, including you, is made up of tiny particles called **molecules**. These in turn are made of **atoms**, which are made of **electrons**, **protons**, and **neutrons**. These particles are **moving** all the time.

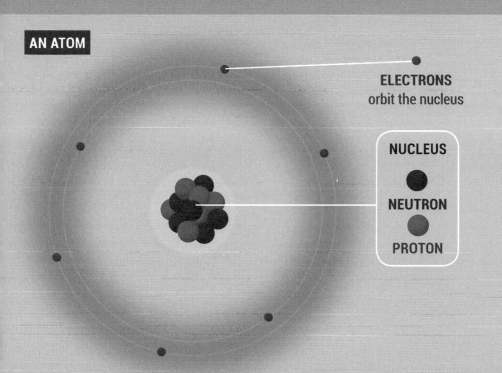

AN ATOM

ELECTRONS
orbit the nucleus

NUCLEUS

NEUTRON

PROTON

Even though an object appears completely still, the particles are constantly moving. We cannot see the movement, even through a microscope, because it is so small. But we can feel its effects when we touch an object.

When we say that an object is HOT, it is because its particles are moving around faster than ours and bumping into ours, GIVING our particles extra energy.

When we feel an object as COLD, it is because its particles are TAKING energy away from our particles as they collide.

Another way we experience heat is when a **CHANGE OF STATE** happens, such as ice melting into water, then turning into steam as it is heated up.

Whether ice, liquid, or steam, water is still made up of the same molecules: hydrogen and oxygen. When the molecules are not moving very fast, they bond together and form a **SOLID** (ice). When they are heated, the bonds weaken and the ice melts into a **LIQUID**. As more heat is applied, the molecules vibrate faster and faster until they form steam (a **GAS**).

STEAM

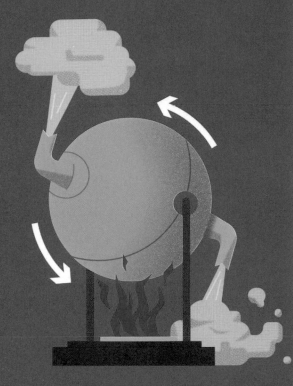

Since ancient times it has been known that steam can be used to generate **motion**. In the first century CE, Hero of Alexandria described a spherical device that would spin when the central container full of water was heated, causing steam to be ejected through nozzles curved in opposite directions. However, Hero never found a good use for his invention.

Watt's steam engine

PISTON

CYLINDER

BOILER

CONDENSER

VACUUM PUMP

How a steam engine works

Steam from a **BOILER** travels into the bottom section of a cylinder, pushing a **PISTON** up. The steam is then sent into the top section of the cylinder, pushing the piston back down and powering the machine. The remaining steam goes into a condenser each time, where it is cooled into water, then carried back to the boiler.

Based on a previous invention by Thomas Newcomen in 1712, **James Watt** developed a machine capable of efficiently converting steam energy into a continuous motion in 1778. The first steam engines were used to pump water out of mines, but they were soon put to many other uses.

HIGH-PRESSURE STEAM

EXHAUST STEAM

A piston is a disk that moves back and forth inside a cylinder, converting the steam's pressure into energy that can turn wheels or run machinery.

1) Steam goes into one end of the cylinder through a valve that stops any escaping.

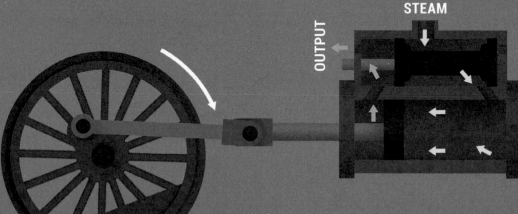

STEAM

VALVE

OUTPUT

2) Steam pushes the piston.

PISTON

3) The steam is now introduced to the other end of the cylinder, pushing the piston back.

STEAM

OUTPUT

4) The back-and-forth movement of the rod attached to the cylinder makes the wheel turn.

Measuring energy

While energy is the capacity to perform work, the **rate** at which this work is performed is called **power**. For example, a strong horse can pull a load faster than a weaker one can, so the strong horse is more powerful.

James Watt measured the power of his steam engine by counting how many horses would be needed to pull the same load the same distance in the same time. So he measured power in units called **HORSEPOWER**. Nowadays, we also use another unit called the **WATT**!

MOVING ON During the **INDUSTRIAL REVOLUTION** in the 18th and 19th centuries, when things began to be made in factories rather than at home, engineers worked out how to make and use energy much more efficiently and powerfully. Steam

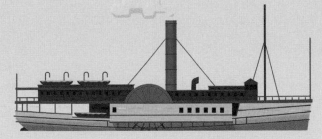

STEAM IN MOTION

As technology improved, steam engines could be made smaller and lighter. This meant they could be used to power vehicles smaller than massive locomotives, such as cars and boats.

PLATFORM 1

engines became more common, making it easier to manufacture goods such as fabrics. **SPEED OF TRAVEL** increased dramatically, and suddenly people could cover large distances faster than ever before. Large numbers of people moved from their homes and settled in formerly remote areas, now connected by transport systems such as railways.

POLLUTION

COAL was the fuel that powered steam engines. Extensive coal mining was needed for new technologies such as steel and cast-iron production. As with wood, burning coal releases the energy stored within it, but it also releases **CARBON DIOXIDE** (a major factor in **CLIMATE CHANGE**) into the air, along with other pollutants that are harmful to living beings.

Transforming and transferring energy

Energy cannot be created or destroyed, so the total amount of energy in the universe doesn't change. Much of our technology is devoted to **transforming energy** from one kind to another or **transferring** it to a different thing.

All energy is either TRANSFERRED from another place or object or TRANSFORMED from another type of energy.

While pedaling, this man is eating a sandwich made from plants that grew by **ABSORBING ENERGY** from the Sun.

Our bodies use chemical reactions in order to **EXTRACT ENERGY** from our food. Oxygen from the air we breathe in breaks up the chemical bonds in the food molecules.

Part of the food's chemical energy is **RELEASED** in the form of heat. This energy has been **TRANSFORMED**.

Another part of the energy from the food **POWERS** the man's muscles, which in turn will power his bicycle.

The energy from this man's legs moving up and down is **TRANSFERRED** to the pedals.

Through the bicycle chain, energy is **TRANSFERRED** from the pedals to the wheels, which **TRANSFORMS** into kinetic energy as the man moves along.

Electric eels and some other animals use electricity to protect themselves against predators, hunt for food, navigate, and communicate. The body of an electric eel contains lines of fluid that let electrically charged atoms called **IONS** pass through.

ELECTRICITY

Around 600 BC, the ancient Greek astronomer Thales of Miletus realized that amber, when rubbed against fur, would **attract** materials such as feathers or hair. What happened was that the fur had taken some particles from the amber, making it and the fur electrically charged, but with opposite charges. Opposite charges **attract** each other, while like charges **repel** each other.

Lightning is a sudden discharge of electricity from the sky, from one cloud to another or to the ground. In 1752, US politician and scientist **BENJAMIN FRANKLIN** demonstrated this by tying a key to a kite string and taking it outside during a thunderstorm. When he felt a spark run from the key to his knuckle, he knew that meant lightning was a form of electricity.

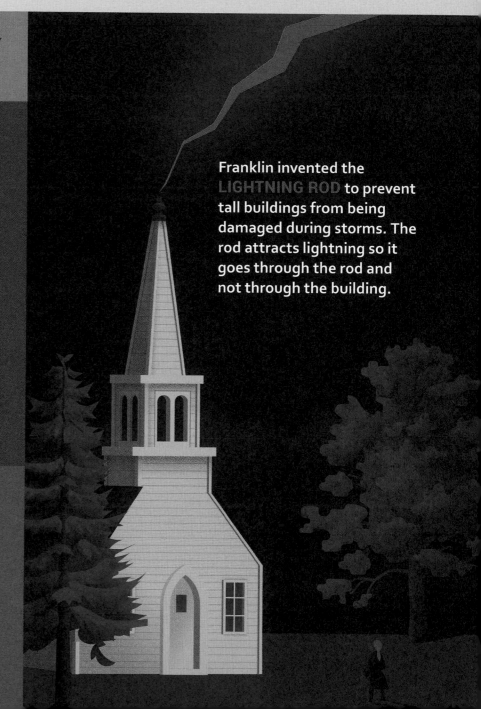

Franklin invented the **LIGHTNING ROD** to prevent tall buildings from being damaged during storms. The rod attracts lightning so it goes through the rod and not through the building.

What is electricity?

When we say that a material is electric, we mean that it has an electric charge. When amber is rubbed, some tiny particles, called **electrons**, are removed. This gives the amber a **static electric charge**, which is stuck there until it can jump to something with the opposite charge.

ELECTRONS are the smallest and lightest particles in the atom. They have a NEGATIVE charge and move fast around the atom. Under the right conditions, they can even jump from atom to atom, traveling relatively long distances: this is called an ELECTRIC CURRENT.

In the center of the atom (**NUCLEUS**), there are larger and heavier particles: **NEUTRONS**, which are not electrically charged, and PROTONS, which carry a POSITIVE electric charge.

An atom with an electron removed or an electron added is electrically charged and is called an ION.

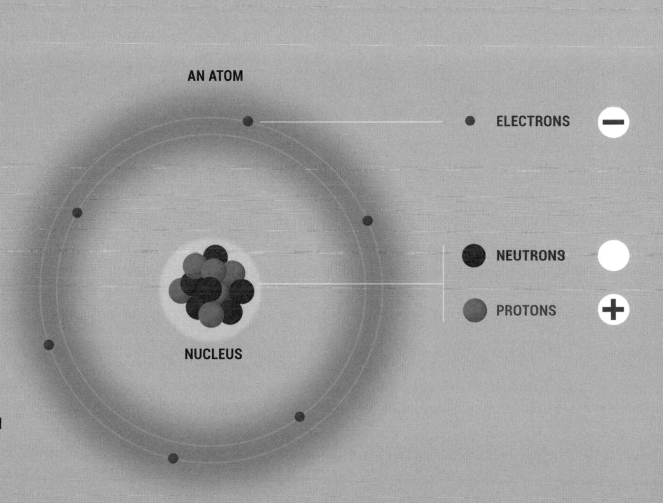

AN ATOM

ELECTRONS

NEUTRONS

PROTONS

NUCLEUS

A flow of electrons from atom to atom is an electric current.

Batteries

Batteries are everywhere: they allow us to store energy and use it whenever we need it. They store **chemical energy**, which can produce an electric current when needed.

To build a battery, you need two chemicals that want to react with each other. You then place a special liquid, called an **ELECTROLYTE**, in between them. The chemicals cannot cross this unless they turn into charged **IONS**.

Nothing happens until you connect both ends of the battery with a wire. The chemicals then swap electrons through it. This turns them into charged ions, so they can now cross the electrolyte, meet, and react. At the same time, the electrons travel through the wire from the **NEGATIVE (−)** end of the battery to the **POSITIVE (+)** end. We now have an electric circuit with a current flowing through it.

Volta's battery

In 1799, **ALESSANDRO VOLTA** created the first battery by stacking layers of copper and zinc in a liquid containing ions (electrolyte). When the two sides of the battery were connected by a cable running outside the liquid, a **CURRENT** of electrons flowed through that cable.

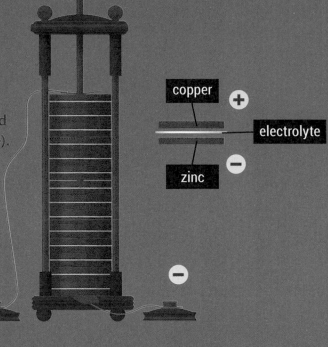

copper ＋
electrolyte
zinc −

＋ −

Modern batteries are based on the same basic design Volta developed, but the liquid electrolyte is replaced with a paste, making them more portable and powerful. When the material in one side of the battery is used up, the battery is empty.

While some batteries can be used only once, others (such as the ones in mobile phones) can be charged again by forcing the electric current to go in reverse.

VOLTA

Napoleon Bonaparte asked Volta to demonstrate his invention in Paris in 1801. To honor the discovery, Napoleon made Volta a count and senator.

CREATING A NETWORK

In 1882, the US entrepreneur and inventor **THOMAS EDISON** set up an **ELECTRIC POWER PLANT** in Pearl Street, New York City. The plant used a steam engine to provide energy to several streets in the city. It was the first step toward the huge **GRID** of electricity **NETWORKS** that have provided energy for the past 150 years to our homes, factories, hospitals, and transport systems.

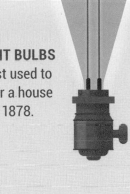

ELECTRIC LIGHT BULBS
These were first used to provide light for a house in the UK in 1878.

POWER PLANT

TRANSFORMER

TRANSMISSION SUBSTATION

Electricity travels from the power plant where it is made to where it is needed via a network of cables and power lines.

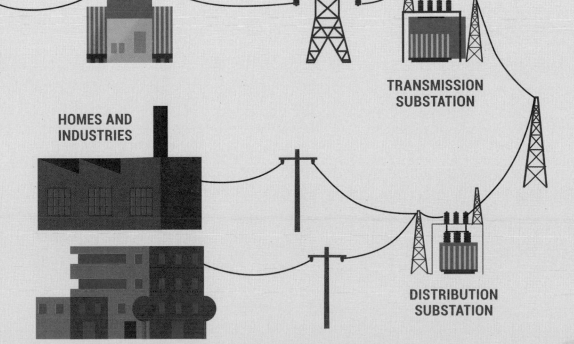

HOMES AND INDUSTRIES

DISTRIBUTION SUBSTATION

Electromagnetism

Thousands of years ago, the ancient Greeks realized that special chunks of stone on the island of **MAGNESIA** were able to **ATTRACT** metallic objects: they called these stones **MAGNETS**.

The Chinese also worked out that metals put in contact with magnets will behave like magnets, even if only for a short time.

In the 19th century, **JAMES CLERK MAXWELL** discovered that **ELECTRIC CURRENTS** also had magnetic properties. This means that moving a magnet will affect an electric current, causing it to curve.

This showed how ELECTRICITY and MAGNETISM were related, and studying them together led to many other scientific discoveries.

Maxwell also realized that LIGHT was an electromagnetic phenomenon, and he predicted the discovery of RADIO WAVES.

Electric motors

Varying the current in an electromagnet can make a nearby magnetic object move. It can make a wheel turn, for example. This is the principle of the **electric** or **induction motor**.

STATOR
A static and permanent row of magnets lining the edge of the motor casing.

COOLING FAN

ROTOR
Usually made of copper wire wound into a coil around an axis. When an electric current flows through the coil, repulsion forces make the shaft spin.

ELECTROMAGNETS

Opposite poles attract each other

Like poles repel each other

Magnets can either REPEL (push away) or ATTRACT each other, depending on which of their ends (or POLES) face each other. Moving one magnet very close to another will make that other magnet move.

Maxwell showed that we can replace either magnet with an ELECTRIC CURRENT: this is called an ELECTROMAGNET. Instead of moving the electromagnet in and out of the way, we can simply switch the electric current on and off, or change its intensity with time.

Running electricity through a wire creates a magnetic field around the wire.

Coiling the wire around a rod creates a stronger magnetic field.

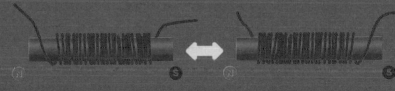

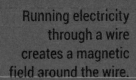

The rod will have north and south magnetic poles.

SHAFT

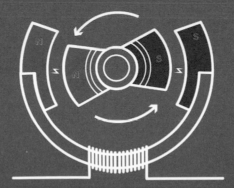

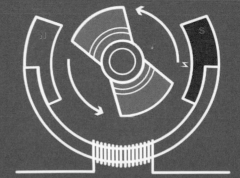

Repulsion effect

OPPOSITE poles ATTRACT and LIKE poles REPEL. When you surround the rod with other magnets, the rod will ROTATE because of the attractive and repulsive forces created. By continually changing the direction of the current, we are able to generate a continuous rotation.

Producing electricity

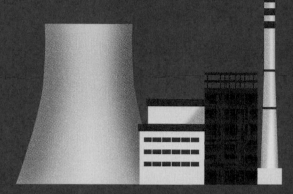

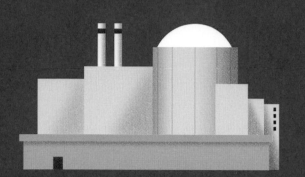

NUCLEAR POWER PLANT

WIND GENERATORS

THERMAL POWER PLANT

The amount of electricity we use has increased dramatically since Edison's time. The way we produce energy has also changed, allowing us to supply the increasing amounts of power our society demands. From coal-burning power plants to dams and nuclear power plants, electricity is usually produced using a **turbine** that converts mechanical motion (such as from wind, water, or steam) into electricity.

DAM

HYDROELECTRICITY

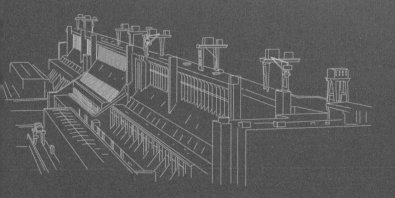

The **THREE GORGES DAM** in China is the world's largest power production facility, with the **ITAIPU DAM** at the border between Brazil and Paraguay a close second. The Itaipu Dam provides many times more electricity than is needed by the whole country of Paraguay, and about a fifth of what Brazil uses. Although dams flood the land, damaging ecosystems and forcing people to leave their homes, once built they do not release much greenhouse gas.

Water flows downhill, speeding up in tunnels and pipes.

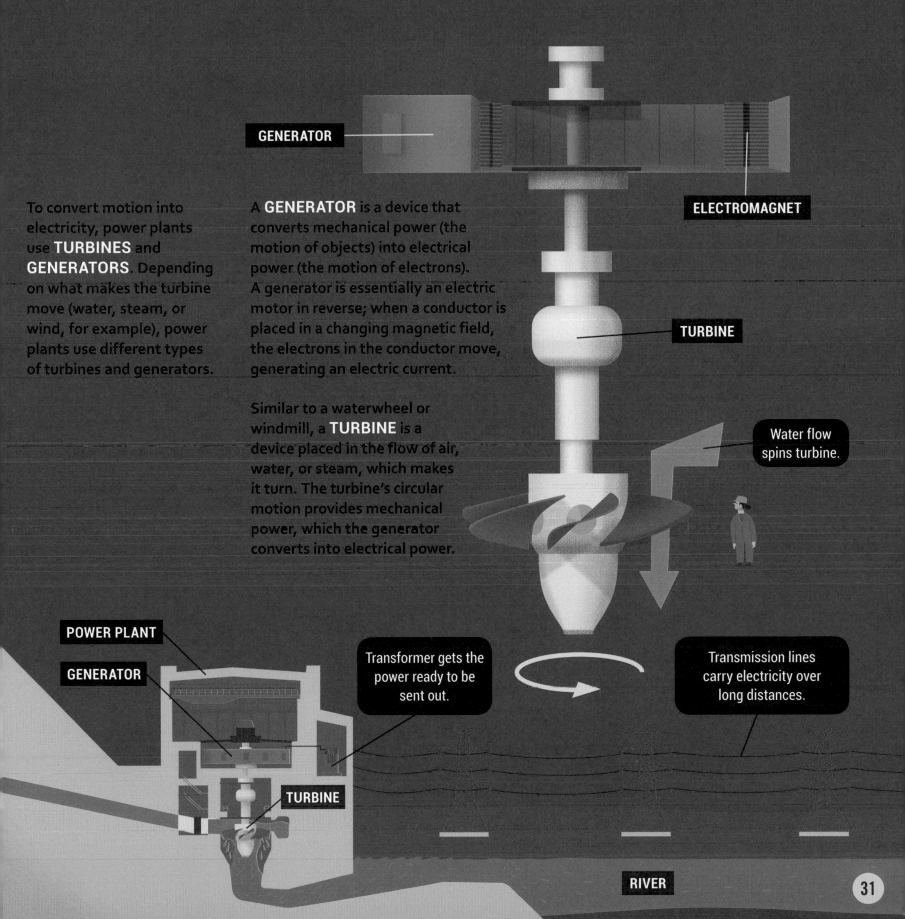

To convert motion into electricity, power plants use **TURBINES** and **GENERATORS**. Depending on what makes the turbine move (water, steam, or wind, for example), power plants use different types of turbines and generators.

A **GENERATOR** is a device that converts mechanical power (the motion of objects) into electrical power (the motion of electrons). A generator is essentially an electric motor in reverse; when a conductor is placed in a changing magnetic field, the electrons in the conductor move, generating an electric current.

Similar to a waterwheel or windmill, a **TURBINE** is a device placed in the flow of air, water, or steam, which makes it turn. The turbine's circular motion provides mechanical power, which the generator converts into electrical power.

GENERATOR

ELECTROMAGNET

TURBINE

Water flow spins turbine.

POWER PLANT

GENERATOR

TURBINE

Transformer gets the power ready to be sent out.

Transmission lines carry electricity over long distances.

RIVER

FOSSIL FUELS

Petroleum, **natural gas**, and **coal** are known as **fossil fuels**. This is because they come from the fossilized remains of dead plants and animals, which have spent millions of years underground under high pressure from the rocks and soil above.

An incredibly long time has to pass between when a plant grows and its remains being dug up from the ground for us to use as fuel. We are now using these fossil fuels too fast for the underground deposits to replenish themselves. Fossil fuels are therefore called **NONRENEWABLE**.

At the rate we currently use fossil fuels, we only have enough left for a few decades at most.

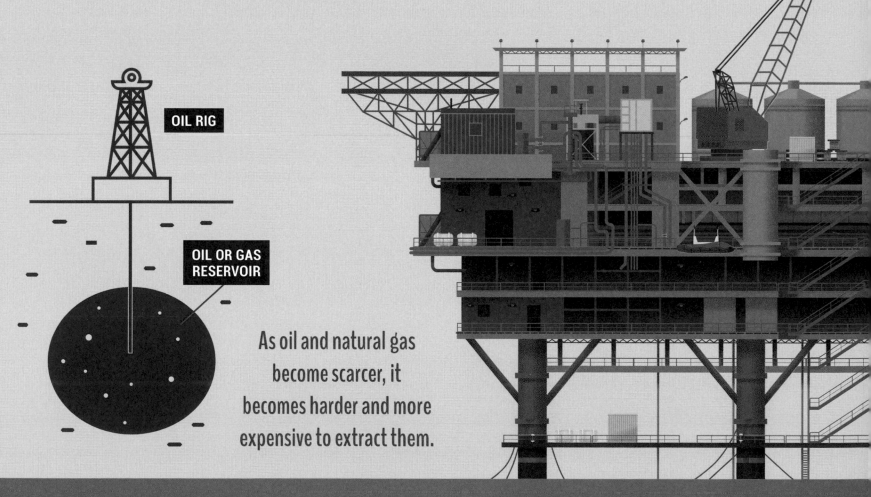

OIL RIG

OIL OR GAS RESERVOIR

As oil and natural gas become scarcer, it becomes harder and more expensive to extract them.

Many oil fields are located deep below the sea bed. Extracting oil and natural gas from them is difficult and requires platforms to be anchored to the sea bed. These are very large, technically advanced, and expensive structures.

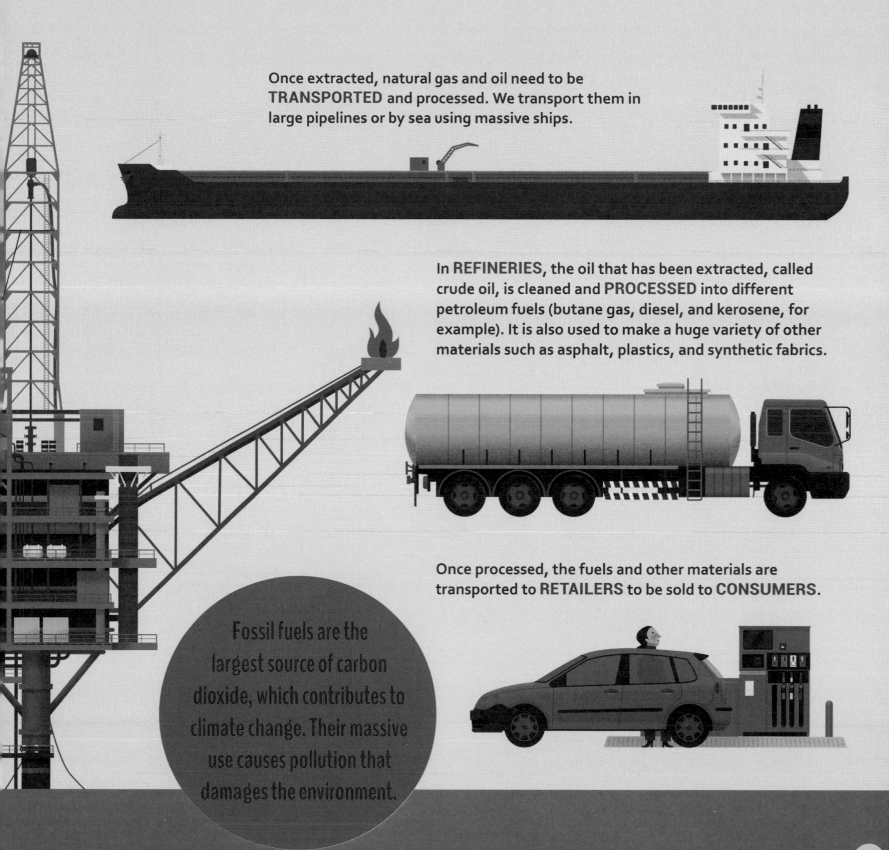

Once extracted, natural gas and oil need to be **TRANSPORTED** and processed. We transport them in large pipelines or by sea using massive ships.

In **REFINERIES**, the oil that has been extracted, called crude oil, is cleaned and **PROCESSED** into different petroleum fuels (butane gas, diesel, and kerosene, for example). It is also used to make a huge variety of other materials such as asphalt, plastics, and synthetic fabrics.

Once processed, the fuels and other materials are transported to **RETAILERS** to be sold to **CONSUMERS**.

Fossil fuels are the largest source of carbon dioxide, which contributes to climate change. Their massive use causes pollution that damages the environment.

Combustion engines

From the first cars to supersonic airplanes, combustion engines have been used to power all sorts of vehicles. While steam engines use water vapor to push pistons, a combustion engine relies on **burning petroleum** mixed with **compressed air**.

Four-stroke engine

FUEL AND AIR

PISTON

CYLINDER

EXHAUST

1) A spark ignites a mixture of fuel and air, creating a hot gas that pushes the piston down. This generates power for the machine and gets the piston moving for the next three strokes.

2) The piston moves up, pushing the burnt gases out.

3) The piston goes down, pulling an air-fuel mixture into the cylinder to get ready for the next cycle.

4) The piston goes up, compressing the mixture in time for the next spark (which is stroke one of the next cycle).

There are now billions of vehicles with combustion engines around the world, affecting how we live our lives.

Jet engines

Most modern airplanes use jet engines. Even though it allows us to fly through the air, the concept of a jet engine is in some ways simpler than that of a combustion engine.

In a jet engine, because the plane is traveling through the sky, there is no need to transmit motion to wheels. The expanding gases can simply be pushed out at the back of the engine, pushing the whole aircraft forward. This means there is no need for a piston, and the fuel and air can be injected continuously, instead of waiting for the right time in the cycle.

For the same reason, the compression of the air is also continuous, and happens as the aircraft flies through the air. The air enters the engine, then gets funneled and compressed by rotating fan blades at the intake side of the engine. These blades are powered by a turbine in the flow of hot gases at the exhaust end of the engine.

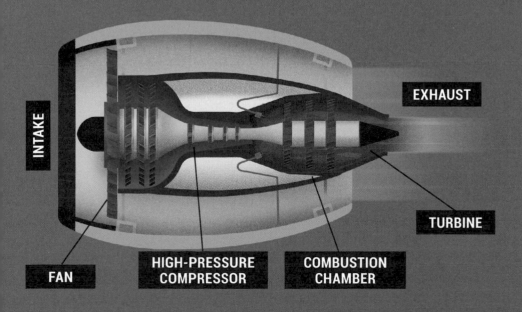

INTAKE

EXHAUST

TURBINE

FAN

HIGH-PRESSURE COMPRESSOR

COMBUSTION CHAMBER

The fastest aircraft

The North American X-15 holds the current world record for the fastest manned aircraft. To reach these speeds, it relied on rockets instead of a jet engine. Its maximum speed was over 4,000 miles per hour. This type of engine is mainly found in military aircraft.

NUCLEAR FISSION

ELECTRON

PROTON

NEUTRON

Nuclear fission is the splitting of a nucleus. We've already discovered that each atom has a nucleus (containing protons and neutrons) with electrons orbiting it. When there are many neutrons and protons inside a nucleus, we call it a heavy nucleus. The number of electrons in an atom is normally equal to the number of protons in the nucleus.

Nuclear fission is when a HEAVY atomic nucleus SPLITS into TWO (OR MORE) LIGHTER nuclei. This process releases a large amount of energy.

The nuclei of some elements are not stable. These nuclei are RADIOACTIVE, meaning they emit energy and particles. This is called RADIATION.

In NATURAL RADIOACTIVITY, fission occurs spontaneously. This means that in certain elements in nature, such as polonium or radium, the atoms can split of their own accord.

In INDUCED FISSION a nucleus is deliberately bombarded, usually with neutrons, so that it becomes unstable and splits, releasing particles (normally more neutrons) and a lot of energy.

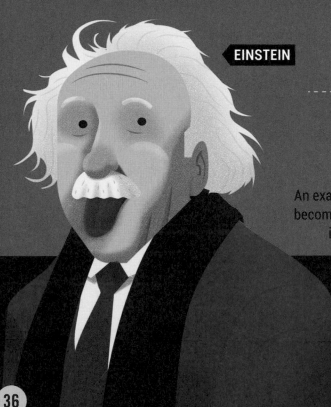

EINSTEIN

1   2   3

An example of INDUCED FISSION occurs when a neutron hits a uranium nucleus (1). The nucleus becomes unstable and splits, releasing more neutrons and energy (2). The released neutrons can in turn collide with other uranium nuclei (3), generating immense amounts of energy.

If you weighed all the particles very precisely before and after fission, you would find that the total mass—or the quantity of matter— afterwards was slightly smaller than it was before. The missing mass has been converted to ENERGY, as calculated by ALBERT EINSTEIN in his famous equation $E = mc^2$, where E is the energy, m is the mass, and c is the speed of light.

A nuclear power plant produces hot steam to rotate a turbine, which in turn generates electricity. The fuel used to create the steam is very special. Instead of a chemical reaction (such as burning coal or natural gas), which changes how atoms are combined within molecules, the nuclear plant relies on fission, which changes how protons and neutrons are combined within an atom's nucleus.

We use NUCLEAR ENERGY in different ways. Atomic bombs are among the most destructive weapons ever, and some military submarines are fueled by an atomic engine. But the main use of nuclear energy is in power plants to produce electricity.

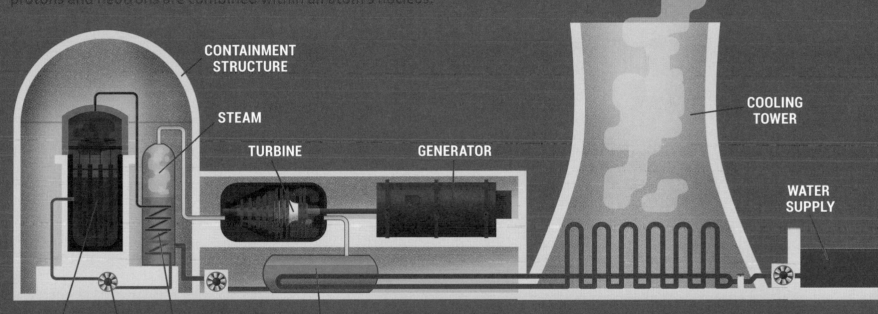

CONTAINMENT STRUCTURE

STEAM

TURBINE

GENERATOR

COOLING TOWER

WATER SUPPLY

NUCLEAR FUEL

PUMP

WATER

CONDENSER (COOLING WATER)

Most nuclear power plants use **URANIUM** nuclei in the fission process. This releases so much energy per atom that relatively small quantities of uranium are needed, and there is enough on the planet for many centuries to come.

While fossil fuels leave greenhouse gases behind as waste, fission leaves RADIOACTIVE waste, which gives off dangerous particles and is active for thousands of years. No perfect solution has been found to this problem, and in the meantime nuclear waste is being kept in temporary storage sites. Catastrophes in power plants, such as Chernobyl in Ukraine and Fukushima in Japan, have also shown the potential risk of nuclear power when accidents happen.

Clean and green energy

Given how fast we burn coal, oil, and natural gas, we may well run out before the end of the century. But we face a bigger problem even before that: burning fossil fuels for a few more decades is likely to change the climate for ever—causing more and more droughts, storms, floods, hurricanes, and famines.

Why do we keep using fossil fuels?

We keep using fossil fuels because that's what we are used to. The **INFRASTRUCTURE** (oil drills, pipelines, refineries, and petrol stations) is already in place, making it easier to use petrol engines instead of investing in new equipment to switch to a new technology.

What energy sources could we use instead?

We will probably need a mix of different energy sources since our current way of life requires an incredible amount of power. When we buy things or travel to places, we use energy. Even when we are sitting at home, our televisions, heating or air conditioning, fridges, and lamps are using energy. And all these items have had to be manufactured using energy and materials.

How can we change our way of life as well as our energy sources?

Some objects and materials cannot be reused, so they should be recycled. This saves energy for manufacturing new ones. It also avoids waste, which doesn't just disappear, but ends up in landfill or in the sea, where it will stay for many hundreds of years.

Electric vehicles

Using electric vehicles can produce fewer greenhouse gases, provided the electricity itself is not generated in a coal-fired plant, but using clean, **RENEWABLE** sources.

Biodiesel

We can actually make fuel out of **PLANTS** to run our vehicles and engines. But we have to be careful that this does not compete with the crops we need to grow for food.

WIND TURBINES

Wind

Wind turbines come in a wide range of shapes and mechanisms, all of them using wind to create a continuous motion and transmit it to a generator that produces electricity. The power of the electricity they output varies as the wind speed changes. Wind turbines can be used to produce electricity for a single building, or they can be connected to an electricity grid.

We can also take advantage of tides and waves to generate energy.

A wind turbine is like a modern windmill. The movement of the wind turns two or three blades attached to the main shaft, which spins a generator to produce electricity.

GEARS transmit the motion of the blades to a shaft that spins much faster, so the generator can work more efficiently.

BLADES

LOW-SPEED SHAFT

HIGH-SPEED SHAFT

GENERATOR

These turbines act like wind generators, using rotor blades to create electricity.

This device uses the up-and-down motion of waves to pump water to a generator.

Some wind turbines are taller than 250yd. Of course, it is not easy to transport and build such massive structures.

NUCLEAR FUSION

Nuclei usually repel each other because of their electric charges. But under massive pressure, they may collide and **fuse** to form a larger nucleus, while releasing a **HUGE** amount of energy. This is called nuclear fusion.

A common **FUSION REACTION** is when two types of hydrogen nuclei, called deuterium and tritium, fuse together to form helium and a neutron.

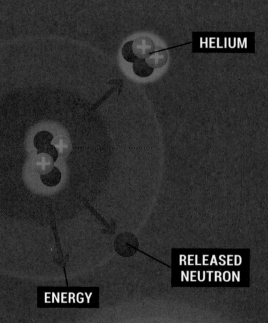

DEUTERIUM
has 1 proton and
1 neutron

TRITIUM
has 1 proton and
2 neutrons

HELIUM

ENERGY

RELEASED NEUTRON

Deuterium and tritium are different versions (isotopes) of hydrogen, which has just 1 proton

This fusion reaction produces a helium atom, a single neutron, and an incredible amount of energy since the mass of the products is different from the mass of the original nuclei (remember Einstein's $E = mc^2$).

Fusion is the energy source of the stars. Our Sun is a large ball of very hot gas (mainly hydrogen and helium).

TOKAMAK
This machine is designed to harness fusion energy.

MAGNETS
Massive superconducting magnets will produce the magnetic fields to create and control plasma, preventing it from reaching the walls.

BLANKET

CRYOSTAT
Ensures an ultra-cool, vacuum environment.

VACUUM VESSEL

PLASMA
This is a hot, ionized gas.

Clean power

The fuel deuterium is found in sea water. It is cheap, abundant, and found around the world. Fusion does not create radioactive waste or greenhouse gases.

Safe power

Unlike fission, which can get out of control, fusion reactions are very difficult to maintain for long enough to produce heat, let alone be dangerous.

Infinite power

It would be an almost eternal energy since we would have enough fuel on the planet for millions of years, taking into account the current energy consumption.

Why are we not already using it?

The difficulty with fusion is to keep the hydrogen at a high enough temperature in a closed space so that the reaction can produce enough heat to keep going. The required temperature, up to 270 million degrees Fahrenheit, will melt any material, so we need to find ways to recreate these "micro-suns" on Earth.

THE ITER PROJECT

In southern France, 35 nations are working together to build the world's largest tokamak to show we can use fusion as a source of energy. It works by introducing just 2g of hydrogen into the vacuum vessel and through a massive magnetic field, confining the plasma so it does not destroy the walls of the reactor. When it reaches the incredible temperature of 270 million degrees Fahrenheit, atoms start to fuse.

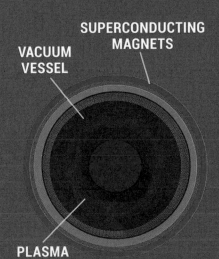

SUPERCONDUCTING MAGNETS

VACUUM VESSEL

PLASMA

Electromagnetic radiation

Visible light is just a tiny part of the large range of **electromagnetic waves** or **radiation** that James Clerk Maxwell identified when he linked electricity with magnetism.

ELECTROMAGNETIC RADIATION travels in **WAVES** (like ripples spreading out on a pond). These waves have different lengths (measured from one peak to the next). **SHORTER** waves move **FASTER** and have **MORE ENERGY**, while **LONGER** waves move **SLOWER** and have **LESS ENERGY**.

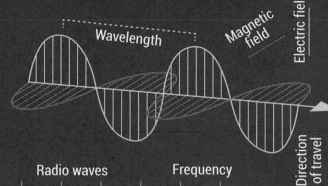

Wavelength

Magnetic field

Electric field

Direction of travel

More energy									Less energy
	Gamma rays	X-rays	UV rays	Infrared rays	Micro-wave	FM	AM	Long radio waves	

Radio waves   Frequency

Shorter wavelengths   Longer wavelengths

We use electromagnetic radiation in many everyday objects.

We can only see waves within this tiny range. This is called **VISIBLE LIGHT** and includes all the colors of the rainbow. There is actually an enormous range of wavelengths beyond visible light. We can't see them, but we can build devices to produce and receive them.

A microwave oven uses MICROWAVES about 4in long to heat up food.

Cell phones also use electromagnetic radiation in the MICROWAVE range.

MORE ENERGETIC electromagnetic waves such as ULTRAVIOLET and X-RAYS are used in hospitals.

INFRARED WAVES about a millionth of a yard long are sent by our remote controls.

TVs and radios receive RADIO WAVES about a yard long through antennae or satellite dishes.

SOLAR ENERGY

Every second, the Sun sends a tremendous amount of energy. All the machines in the world only require as much power as one percent of the Sun's rays hitting the Sahara Desert.

This means that the Sun could potentially provide for all our energy needs, as long as we can **STORE** it for use at night or on cloudy days, or **SEND** it from the sunny side of the planet to the side where it is night.

Ancient Greek mathematician Archimedes is said to have used curved mirrors to focus the Sun's rays on a single point and set fire to the ships of Roman invaders.

Like Archimedes, we can use a magnifying glass to focus the Sun's rays and set light to a piece of paper. (Ask an adult to help if you want to try this!)

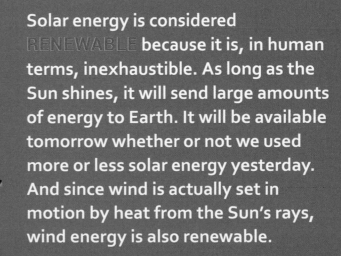

Solar energy is considered RENEWABLE because it is, in human terms, inexhaustible. As long as the Sun shines, it will send large amounts of energy to Earth. It will be available tomorrow whether or not we used more or less solar energy yesterday. And since wind is actually set in motion by heat from the Sun's rays, wind energy is also renewable.

Solar energy provides energy for life on Earth, and we use it to heat our houses, but there are other ways to convert the Sun's rays into useful energy.

WATER TANK

The Sun heats water in this bendy pipework.

Solar water heating

Instead of using electricity or burning fossil fuels that have stored the Sun's energy, we can use the Sun's rays directly by designing houses that are better at retaining its heat. We can also use sunlight to heat the water we use in our showers.

The Sun's rays will be there for us to use everyday, as long as the Sun has enough fuel, which should be the case for at least five billion years.

CONCENTRATED SOLAR POWER

In **SOLAR THERMAL PLANTS**, curved mirrors concentrate the Sun's rays on a water vessel. This creates steam that spins a turbine and generates electricity.

Some other liquids work better than simple water. For instance, chemicals similar to table salt can be heated until they melt. These enable the plant to retain the heat until long after the Sun has gone down, allowing us to **STORE** its power for use at night or on cloudy days.

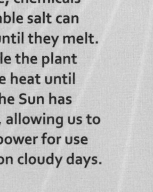

PHOTOVOLTAICS

Satellites use photovoltaic cells to get energy.

PHOTOVOLTAIC CELL

A **solar panel** is made up of electronic devices called **photovoltaic cells**. Particles of light (light can behave both as a wave and as particles known as a **photons**) give their energy directly to the electrons in the photovoltaic cell to create an electric current.

Manufacturing costs for solar panels have gone down so much that photovoltaic electricity now often costs less than electricity from coal. The same is true of electricity from wind turbines.

Solar panels can be installed on rooftops, in remote areas not connected to an electricity network, and even built into portable equipment. To produce large amounts of electricity for cities or factories, they can be installed in rows on the ground or on barges floating on lakes.

Solar panels can be made to turn during the day in order to capture more of the Sun's rays as it moves across the sky.

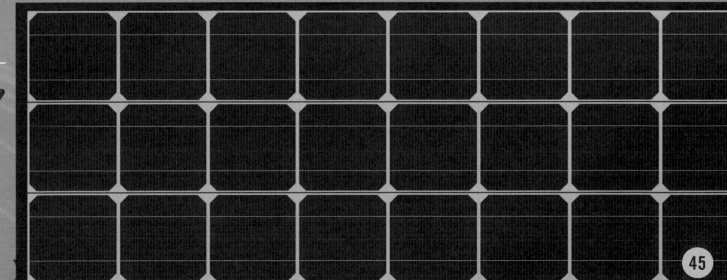

SOLAR PANEL

SMART GRIDS

For a **sustainable future**, we need to change not only how we produce energy but also how we **use** and **share** it.

In the traditional way of producing energy, coal-fired power plants can be turned up or down as needed. As we rely more on solar and wind power, which vary depending on the time of day and the weather, we will need to build a more flexible electricity network. Electricity production and distribution will become more local, with more and smaller power generators, and will need to be smarter, using software to predict demand.

FUSION POWER PLANT

WIND TURBINE

FARM

OPERATION CENTER

Use of energy is studied so it can be provided to meet demand.

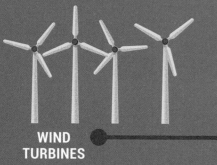

WIND TURBINES

STADIUM

SOLAR PANELS

ENERGY STORAGE PLANT

TRANSMISSION AND DISTRIBUTION

SOLAR PANELS

SOLAR PANELS

INDUSTRIAL CLUSTER

1   2   3

CITY

EXPLORING SPACE

To travel to other planets, we need sources of energy that last a long time and allow us to send humans to Mars and explore beyond the Solar System.

SPACE PROBE

A solar sail is an extremely light mirrorlike material that can be spread out from a satellite, in the same way a sail can be spread out from a sailboat.

The sails use SUNLIGHT instead of wind. The light particles that bounce off the sail give it enough of a push to set it in motion.

SOLAR SAIL
This spans half a mile or more.

Solar sails will allow us to send space probes to explore outer space.

ION DRIVE

CARGO HOLD

SHUTTLE

843C2   082B   94XX

Ion drives use an ELECTRIC FIELD to push electrically charged particles from its tail end. This creates a forward thrust in the same way that a jet engine does.

It will allow us to go farther, faster, and with much less fuel than current engines.

Ion drives could help humans live elsewhere in the Solar System.

Button Books

First published 2020 by Button Books, an imprint of Guild of Master Craftsman Publications Ltd, Castle Place, 166 High Street, Lewes, East Sussex, BN7 1XU, UK. Illustrations © Eduard Altarriba, 2020. Copyright in the Work © GMC Publications Ltd, 2020. ISBN 978 1 78708 049 2. Distributed by Publishers Group West in the United States.
A catalog record for this book is available from the British Library. Publisher: Jonathan Bailey. Production: Jim Bulley and Jo Pallett. Senior Project Editor: Wendy McAngus. Text: Steve Evans, Johannes Hirn, and Veronica Sanz. Technical Consultant: Florence Gadsby. Managing Art Editor: Gilda Pacitti. Color origination by GMC Reprographics. Printed and bound in China.